SOUNDBITES

Groups, Bands and Orchestras

Roger Thomas

Heinemann
LIBRARY

www.heinemann.co.uk/library
Visit our website to find out more information about Heinemann Library books.

To order:
☎ Phone 44 (0) 1865 888066
📄 Send a fax to 44 (0) 1865 314091
💻 Visit the Heinemann Bookshop at www.heinemann.co.uk/library to browse our catalogue and order online.

First published in Great Britain by Heinemann Library, Halley Court, Jordan Hill, Oxford, OX2 8EJ, a division of Reed Educational and Professional Publishing Ltd.
Heinemann is a registered trademark of Reed Educational and Professional Publishing Ltd.

OXFORD MELBOURNE AUCKLAND
JOHANNESBURG BLANTYRE GABORONE
IBADAN PORTSMOUTH NH (USA) CHICAGO

Designed by Paul Davies and Associates
Originated by Ambassador Litho Ltd.
Printed at Wing King Tong in Hong Kong

ISBN 0 431 13075 2 (hardback)   ISBN 0 431 13082 5 (paperback)
06 05 04 03 02   06 05 04 03 02
10 9 8 7 6 5 4 3 2   10 9 8 7 6 5 4 3 2 1

British Library Cataloguing in Publication Data

Thomas, Roger, 1956-
    Groups, bands and orchestras. - (Soundbites)
    1.Musical groups - Juvenile literature
    I.Title
    784

Acknowledgements
The Publishers would like to thank the following for permission to reproduce photographs: Christian Him: Pg.16; Corbis: Pg.10, Pg.26; Echo City: Pg.29; GetMusic.com: Pg.28; Hulton Getty: Pg.24; Lebrecht Picture Library: Pg.4, Pg.7, Pg.8, Pg.18, Pg.20, Pg.23; Panos Pictures: Pg.5; Photodisc: Pg.19; Redferns: Pg.6, Pg.9, Pg.11, Pg.12, Pg.13, Pg.14, Pg.17, Pg.21, Pg.22, Pg.27; Retna: Pg.15; Sally Greenhill: Pg.25.

Cover photograph reproduced with permission of Redferns/Steve Gillett.

Our thanks to John Ranck for his comments in the preparation of this book.

Every effort has been made to contact copyright holders of any material reproduced in this book. Any omissions will be rectified in subsequent printings if notice is given to the publishers.

Contents

Any words appearing in bold, **like this**, are explained in the Glossary

Introduction

People have been gathering together to make music for as long as history has been recorded, and probably for much longer than that. Unlike many other activities, such as eating and sleeping, music does not at first appear essential to human life. However, it is impossible to escape the basic elements that go to make up music: **pitch**, **dynamics** (whether a sound is loud or soft), **timbre** and **rhythm**. We experience all these sounds of everyday life.

Where does music come from?

Our basic understanding of music comes from the ways in which we process important information about the world around us. Most natural sounds have a clear pitch that we use to gain information about the sounds themselves. For example, when we hear a dog bark, we know that if the bark is high-pitched, the dog is probably a small one, whereas a low-pitched bark probably means a big dog. The timbre of a sound (the mixture of elements that make a sound recognizable) tells us even more – for example, it allows us to tell the difference between the sound of a broken glass and the sound of a broken china plate. Rhythm has always played a crucial role in human life. Our understanding of rhythm tells us if someone's heart rate and breathing are regular, helps us to walk and run effectively, to chew our food safely and to do physical work efficiently (imagine trying to hammer a nail into wood without using a regular rhythm).

Today's music making developed from early human survival skills, which used the ability to interpret sounds to help with hunting and protection from predators.

These Aboriginal Australians are using sticks that are stamped on the ground. This kind of group percussion playing is thousands of years old and evolved from making loud noises to frighten away predators.

'Pre-music' in prehistory

All these kinds of information were essential for the survival and development of human beings during **prehistoric** times. A high-pitched animal cry could mean a small animal that could be hunted for food, whereas a low-pitched cry could mean a larger animal, possibly a dangerous **predator** to be avoided. The loudness of the sound helped show how close the animal was. The simple sound of raindrops could mean there would soon be pools of fresh drinking water, whereas the complex timbres of a thunderstorm pointed to possible danger. The irregular breathing of an animal wounded by a hunter showed that it was becoming weak and would soon provide fresh food. This ability to recognize and understand sound eventually developed into music.

From life into art

The visual arts began with cave-paintings that preserved actual events, such as hunting, and literature began with factual record keeping. Music also developed from a set of practical skills. Early occupations, such as hunting, gathering food and protection from predators worked better when done in groups, therefore, the music that evolved from these activities also developed as a group activity.

The first musical groups

No musician is ever alone

We tend to see groups of musicians and musicians making music on their own as very different. However, all music, whether a **solo** performance, someone making music on a home computer or even a baby playing with a rattle, involves many people. For example, a single cellist playing an unaccompanied piece may not be a 'group' in the usual sense. However, he or she relies on the composer who wrote the music, the publisher that printed the music, the teacher(s) who taught him or her how to listen to music, how to read a **score** and how to play the instrument, the instrument-maker who made the instrument (not to mention the instrument's original inventor), and so on. Then there are the people who taught all the others how to compose, teach and build cellos, and the people who taught them, as well as the influence of all the other musicians that those involved may have listened to. All music is the result of the efforts of a large number of people. A solo performer is perhaps best thought of as the single playing member of the 'group' described above, a group that may extend all over the world and across history.

A solo musician is part of a much larger group – a group of all the different people involved, from the inventor of the instrument, to the composer, to the person who taught the musician to play.

Making music together

The first human beings used their voices and the objects around them to make sounds, making them all 'performers'. It is likely that the earliest music making began in **prehistoric** times as a group activity – for the same reason people started doing other things in groups: it worked better. Hunting was easier when several hunters were involved, food gathering was more thorough when a whole group worked on a single area at once, and so on. It would have been more effective when a whole group of hunters used their voices and other noises to chase **prey**, or to frighten away **predators**. As true music began to develop, the power of several voices or early **percussionists** using branches and rocks, when compared to the efforts of a single person, would have been very clear. It is likely that the earliest group music involved some form of worship celebration. If we look at today's religious gatherings, songs for special occasions (such as your friends singing 'Happy Birthday' to you) and football chants, we can see that these ideas have stayed with us.

Formal music

Some of the earliest formal group music that we know existed is shown on ancient carvings from the ancient Sumerian civilization, dating from around 3000 BC. We know that music was seen as important in this society, because the musicians are shown playing for a royal official and because this picture was used on the standard of the Sumerian city of Ur.

This ancient Sumerian standard is one of the earliest known illustrations of group music making.

Orchestras

It is reasonable to assume that the idea of organized groups of musicians is as old as music itself. People were making music in groups well before the invention of purpose-built musical instruments. In the **West**, the term 'orchestra' has come to mean a large group of musicians playing a variety of instruments.

Early orchestras

The orchestra as we now know it did not evolve for purely musical reasons. The word itself comes from the Greek word *orkhestra*, which means a space in front of a theatre stage (used by singers and dancers involved in a play). When **opera** first began in Europe, during the early 17th century, the singers were accompanied by a small group of musicians. Composers then realised that the music could also be used to help describe the thoughts and emotions of the characters onstage. This led to more and more instruments being used in the orchestra. Identical or similar instruments were grouped into sections. This happened about the same time as the invention of the violin, which was well-suited to this new kind of large instrumental group. It had a louder and clearer sound than its predecessor, the viol. The Italian composer Claudio Monteverdi (1567–1643) had an orchestra that was made up of stringed instruments of various sizes together with a harp.

Today's orchestras are generally directed by a conductor, who directs the music and keeps time with a baton, although this role only really developed in the early 19th century.

The orchestra progresses

By the mid-17th century, the French court composer Jean-Baptiste Lully (1632–1687) introduced woodwinds to his orchestra. However, it was not until the beginning of the 18th century that brass instruments began to be used regularly in orchestras. Even then, because communication between various countries was much slower than today, ideas about which instruments should be included varied from place to place. During the 19th century, new instrument-making skills enabled the production of many redesigned brass and woodwind instruments which would stay **in tune** and which could be played in different **keys**. This also led to the orchestral music of the time becoming much more sophisticated.

The orchestra today

The modern Western orchestra is very similar to that of the 19th century, with a range of instruments that enable the group to play music from several centuries. A typical orchestra will include violins (usually in two sections), violas, cellos, double **basses**, flutes, clarinets, oboes, bassoons, horns, trumpets, trombones, a tuba, **timpani** and other percussion. There are also smaller chamber orchestras, often consisting only of violins, violas, cellos and basses. The term orchestra is also used to describe large musical **ensembles** in other cultures, such as the gamelan orchestras of Bali and Java.

Chamber groups and small instrumental ensembles

Chamber music

'Chamber' is an old word for room, so 'chamber music' simply means music which can be played in an ordinary room rather than a concert hall. Today, the term is usually used to describe any instrumental music written for a group that is smaller than a full-scale orchestra. Chamber **ensembles** (the word ensemble means together) can combine many different instruments. Here are just a few examples:

- THE STRING QUARTET is one of the best-known types of chamber group. It consists of two violins, a viola and a cello. A great deal of music is written for this very popular type of group.
- THE STRING TRIO consists of two violins (or occasionally a violin and a viola) and a cello. It is traditionally seen as difficult to write music for the string trio as, unlike the string quartet, there is usually no viola to play the middle notes between the violins and the cello.
- THE PIANO TRIO usually is made up of a violin, a cello and a piano or other keyboard (often a harpsichord). This is a versatile grouping with a wide **repertoire**.

This string quartet is made up of two violins a viola and a cello.

Small, classical groups are central to many other musical cultures, such as that of India, where great emphasis is placed on individual **virtuosity**.

- WIND ENSEMBLES come in many sizes and can have a wide variety of different woodwind instruments. The French horn is often the only brass instrument included, because its **muted**, gentle **tone** blends well with woodwind instruments, such as the flute or clarinet.
- THE SAXOPHONE QUARTET consists of a **soprano**, an **alto**, a **tenor** and a **baritone** saxophone. The saxophone quartet is found both in classical music and **contemporary** jazz.
- THE SONATA is generally seen more as a musical form than a type of group. However, it usually refers specifically to a **composition** for one string or wind instrument plus a piano (or harpsichord in the case of some earlier sonatas). Sonatas written for the piano or other keyboard instruments are generally **solo** pieces.

Other chamber groups

There are many other types in classical music, often mixing a variety of instruments. There is a rough equivalent to chamber music within jazz. The clarinettist Jimmy Guiffre led a group consisting of clarinet, piano and double **bass**, playing a reflective, highly-structured form of music which became referred to as chamber jazz.

Choirs and vocal groups

Singing is one of the oldest ways of making music and it is without a doubt one of the earliest forms of organized music (see pages 6–7). It is also the only form of music making that does not need access to any technology (even the simplest musical instruments need some kind of tool to make them).

Gospel choirs are one of the musical traditions which have grown out of religious worship.

How choirs and vocal groups are put together

Within any **vocal** group the singers are usually divided up into different singing parts according to the **pitch** and **range** of their voices. In a **Western** choir, these voices are (from highest to lowest): **soprano** (usually female, although there are also boy sopranos), **treble** (usually boys), **contralto** (female), **alto** (female), **tenor** (male), **baritone** (male), **bass** (male). There is also a male voice called counter-tenor, which is an artificially high voice used in some early vocal music.

Singing and worship

Singing has always been an important part of religious worship. Group singing multiplies the power of a single voice many times, adding strength to the message of the the worshippers.

Many forms of worship have **choral** traditions. Early Christian vocal music was called plainchant, because it was a very simple, unornamented style (plain) with no instrumental accompaniment (-chant). It was believed that if the music was complex and instruments were used, this would take away from the seriousness of the act of worship. In other cultures, including Native American, Aboriginal Australian and Hindu, it is also felt that music in religious ceremonies should be simple and direct.

The vocal tradition in the Christian church now includes both a choir and congregational singing. This includes group singing on two levels: there is a trained group of singers leading the singing, joined by a much larger group whose abilities will vary.

Cross-cultural choirs

Perhaps because singing is such a universal activity, there is a great deal of interest in the choral traditions of different cultures. One example is Zulu choral music, which combines **close-harmonies** with African **rhythms**. Another example is the unusual Bulgarian choral tradition that, due to the fact that the male population was often away at war, developed with a particular emphasis on women's voices.

Community choirs

In many countries throughout the world, there is a tradition of amateur choirs whose members come from from the local area. These are both a rich source of music making and a social focus for the members. This extends into other vocal forms – from **opera** through to barbershop (the unaccompanied close-harmony singing of popular songs). Choirs may also be associated with particular orchestras.

Barbershop vocal groups perform close-harmony versions of popular songs.

Rock bands

These days it is possible to find rock bands playing at every level of performance, from teenagers playing in a garage to massive stadium concerts. However, during its early history, playing rock music to any high standard often seemed an impossible dream for many musicians.

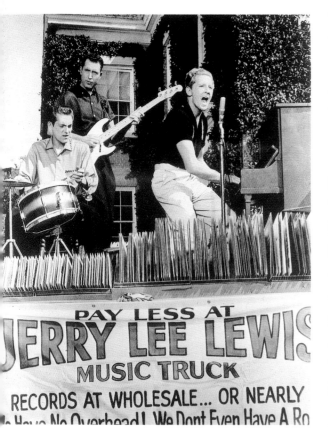

PAY LESS AT
JERRY LEE LEWIS
MUSIC TRUCK
RECORDS AT WHOLESALE... OR NEARLY
Have No Overhead! We Dont Even Have A Ro

Instrumentation was very basic in early rock 'n' roll.

The roots of rock instrumentation

Rock music developed from a variety of popular American musics, including country music, dance band music, jazz and blues. Most of the musics which preceded it were relatively undemanding in terms of the instruments they required – usually inexpensive guitars, fiddles, harmonicas, brass instruments and so on, which could often be bought cheaply. This tradition has been preserved in various forms of American folk music, such as Cajun, for example, in which the only percussion instrument is a triangle.

The invention of **amplified** guitars and bass guitars was originally intended to make these instruments easier to hear in dance bands. However, it soon became clear that it allowed a much smaller group to perform to a large audience. Equally importantly, it allowed the players to use the characteristics of amplified sound to give rock music a special feel. Prior to this, the drum kit had developed from a collection of assorted percussion instruments used in the theatre into a sophisticated, purpose-built instrument. The record and broadcasting industries were progressing during the same period, making the marriage of rock music and technology inevitable.

Rock instruments today

For the first generation of rock musicians, quality instruments were few in number and very expensive. Today, instrument technology is both far better and far cheaper. The core of a modern rock band will usually include:

- one or more GUITARISTS, who will generally use electric instruments played through amplifiers
- a BASSIST, typically playing an electric **bass** guitar through an amplifier
- a DRUMMER, playing a purpose-built kit consisting of a snare and bass drum, cymbals and snareless, **semi-pitched drums** (called tom-toms, or just toms).

Many bands also have a KEYBOARD PLAYER. Today, in addition to piano or the electronic organ, there is a wide variety of sophisticated electronic keyboards.

SINGING may involve a lead singer and possibly backing singers as well. They will use microphones and a large amplification system called a PA (public address) system.

A HORN SECTION of saxophones and brass instruments, a PERCUSSIONIST and a **DJ** (who will add sounds from vinyl records) may also be involved.

Lenny Kravitz is supported by electric guitars and the whole performance is amplified.

15

Jazz groups

The instruments used in jazz originated with those used in military and marching bands. However, the music has developed continuously since its beginnings early in the 20th century. Today, most instruments in existence have been put to use in the performance of jazz music at one time or another – including, in the case of one musician named Rufus Harley, the bagpipes! However, there are some instruments which are much more common in jazz today than others.

The main instruments of a jazz group

Underpinning the music of a typical jazz group from every period, the **RHYTHM** SECTION traditionally consists of piano, drums and double **bass** or bass guitar. The section is so named to distinguish it from the 'front line' of **melody** instruments. The GUITAR may be used as part of the rhythm section in larger bands, or as a front-line instrument in smaller groups.

REED INSTRUMENTS, including the various sizes of saxophone and clarinet, are among the most important instruments in a jazz group, because they tend to play most of the main themes and melodies.

BRASS INSTRUMENTS, usually the trumpet and trombone and occasionally the gentler-**toned** flugelhorn, were used in jazz before the saxophone and have kept their importance.

A typical jazz quartet consists of a saxophone, electric guitar, bass guitar and drum kit.

Instrumental innovations in jazz

Jazz is a music founded on experimentation and jazz musicians are always looking for new instrumental ideas.

ELECTRONIC KEYBOARDS of various kinds are now well established in jazz. These were preceded by the ELECTRIC ORGAN and the ELECTRIC PIANO – both electro-mechanical (part electronic, part mechanical) instruments. Modern **digital** keyboards offer a far wider variety of sounds.

OTHER STRINGED INSTRUMENTS, even the harp, are occasionally used in jazz. Chief among these is the violin, which was central to early **acoustic swing** music and which, with the use of **amplification**, is often used in modern jazz.

OTHER BRASS INSTRUMENTS, including the tuba, the French horn and instruments normally used in marching bands, such as the **tenor** horn, are sometimes included in jazz arrangements. The sousaphone, a very large type of bass tuba, was often used as the bass instrument in early jazz.

TUNED PERCUSSION is found in jazz in the form of the vibraphone. It consists of tuned metal bars with **tube resonators** underneath, with a gentle **tremolo** being added to its sound by small motorized fans at the bottom of the tubes.

LATIN PERCUSSION, consisting of **congas**, **bongos**, **timbales**, **cowbells**, **woodblocks** and many hand percussion instruments, is widely used in both Latin-based jazz and in other forms.

Innovative contemporary jazz orchestras can include all sorts of combinations of instruments.

17

Military and marching bands

The armed forces in most countries have military bands. These were originally used on the battlefield to provide signals which could be heard above the fighting. However, they developed into sophisticated musical units which are often used for ceremonies, parades and for entertaining the public. Drums, brass and woodwind are the main instruments in these bands. Many instruments were originally invented or adapted for use in military bands. Ex-military musicians have brought their knowledge into **civilian** life, which in turn has led to the creation of marching bands in schools, colleges and local communities. Like choirs, these bands are often an important social focus in community life.

The history of the modern marching band is strongly associated with the work of the American composer and bandleader John Philip Sousa (1854–1932), whose expertise resulted in his band touring the world in 1910. Since then, many different instruments have been used in these bands. These include:

• WOODWIND INSTRUMENTS, including the piccolo, flute, clarinet, **alto** and **tenor** saxophone, oboe and bassoon.

The American marching band tradition is a thriving musical culture.

- BRASS INSTRUMENTS of the types also found in symphony orchestras, such as the trumpet, trombone and French horn.
- SPECIALIZED BRASS INSTRUMENTS, many of which have been developed specifically for use in military and marching bands. These include the marching tuba (which, unlike the orchestral tuba, is carried on the shoulder), the bugle (which is also still used as a signalling instrument), the cornet (which is related to the trumpet), the mellophone (which has a trumpet-like shape but which is in fact related to the French horn) and the euphonium (a type of small tuba).
- DRUMS, including snare drums (often known by their original name of side drums, due to the position in which they are carried for marching), tenor drums, tom-toms (often in multiple sets) and **bass** drums (often several of varied **pitches**).
- OTHER PERCUSSION, including cymbals and lyre bells (essentially a **glockenspiel** mounted on a lyre-shaped frame).

Different approaches

In the UK there are several interesting variations on the idea of the marching band. Scottish military bands, for instance, traditionally consist of drums and Highland bagpipes. More unusual in the early 21st century, are the marching **kazoo** bands that were popular in the United States where the instrument was invented in 1850, and in some parts of the UK. The musicians played simple kazoos (or 'tommy talkers') which were often fitted with a trumpet-like bell, or adapted by their owners to resemble traditional band instruments such as trombones. Marching kazoo bands used to be referred to locally as 'jazz bands', to the confusion of visiting jazz fans, who would attend their performances expecting something quite different.

The kazoo is a very simple instrument to play.

Folk groups

The usual definition of folk music is music that has its origins in popular culture rather than as an art form produced by professional composers and musicians. However, sometimes, there is no real distinction between folk music and art music. Some cultures see music as something to take part in rather than as a form of entertainment that musicians present to an audience. At the same time, there are many full-time, professional folk musicians, who make music using folk forms. It is also hard to generalize about the instruments used in folk music worldwide, as these will be determined by the instruments **indigenous** to each culture.

However, there are some elements that are constant. The instruments used in folk music are usually relatively simple and readily available. For example, there is no folk music for the pipe organ, which is a large instrument usually installed in a building. There is, however, a great deal of folk music played on the violin (or fiddle), because the instrument is portable and need not be expensive. Despite the fact that both the violin and the cello share links with **Western** classical music, there is no tradition of playing folk music on the cello, presumably because it is larger and usually more expensive.

A traditional folk group from Ireland. The fiddle and the bodhran are important in Irish folk music.

The Irish band The Corrs are an electric 'folk-rock' group. Their music mingles modern rock with traditional folk sounds.

Folk instruments in the West

Instruments traditionally linked to folk groups in Western culture include the following:

- FRETTED INSTRUMENTS, including the **acoustic** guitar, banjo, mandolin, mandola and **bouzouki**, are among the most widely seen instruments in folk music today. These instruments come from many different countries, showing how folk music is becoming increasingly international.
- WIND INSTRUMENTS, such as tin whistles and flutes are also important. There is also a strong tradition of folk bagpipes in many cultures.
- PERCUSSION instruments – typical examples are frame drums, such as the Irish **bodhran** and rattling and clapping instruments, such as the bones, which are flat sticks of bone or wood that are clicked between the fingers.
- HOME-MADE INSTRUMENTS are also found, such as a pair of spoons used as clappers or a pottery bottle blown across the neck to make bass notes.
- BELLOWS INSTRUMENTS, such as the **concertina**, are found in the folk music of both Europe and the USA.
- The VOICE remains one of the most important elements of folk music. For many centuries folk songs have served as an important form of popular entertainment and also as a way of voicing concerns. Folk songs often tell stories of love, war, humour or some **fantastical** event, but there are also many folk songs that express discontent with, for example, a country's politics.

Groups worldwide

Every culture has its own tradition of group music-making. The origins and traditions of these groups can differ widely. The following examples from various cultures across the world show this **diversity**:

- INDIA: One example of Indian vocal music is *qawwali*, a tradition of songs which are often presented formally to audiences, but which can cover very down-to-earth subjects, such as love and marriage. A *qawwali* group will typically have a lead singer, a chorus of accompanying singers and some instrumentalists.

- SCOTLAND: The pipe band is very much associated with Scottish music. Consisting of Highland bagpipes and drums, these bands are generally attached to military regiments and often give public performances during parades and other events.
- THE SOUTHERN USA: The Cajun community is descended from a group of French-speaking settlers, so the traditional Cajun songs are usually sung in French. Typically, the instruments used are fiddle, accordion and triangle.
- CUBA: The Cuban **samba** tradition is nurtured by 'samba schools', highly competitive trained bands that take part in parades and competitions. The bands use Latin percussion

The bagpipes give a unique sound to Scottish pipe bands.

Steel bands are traditionally West-Indian bands that use tempered oil drums (though these days the drums are usually specially made in a factory).

instruments, and a variety of percussion instruments unique to this tradition. They include the *bomba* (a deep-toned drum), the *tamborim* and the *pandeiro* (two types of frame drum).

- RUSSIA: The balalaika is a traditional Russian **lute**-like instrument, with a distinctive triangular body. A tradition arose for assembling large balalaika orchestras using instruments of various sizes (including a large **bass** instrument which has to be rested on a spike).

- THE WEST INDIES, THE UK AND ELSEWHERE: The steel band, which originated in Trinidad, has a unique and distinctive sound. The steel pans played by the musicians were originally made by **tempering** old oil drums, but today such instruments tend to be made in factories. A steel band uses several different types of pan, with various **pitch ranges**. The drums are named according to their sound, pitch or function within the band: **rhythm** drums, ping-pong, second pan, cello, guitar and bass drums.

Endless variety

These examples are only a very few of the thousands of different musical groupings that exist in **Western** and non-Western cultures – but the desire to make music in a group is common to all societies.

Informal groups

While there are now any number of other sources of music, people of all ages still choose to make music in a group just for fun. The music usually takes the form of singing and, interestingly, may enhance an already happy occasion or lift the spirits of the singers if they are in some sort of difficult situation. One memorable example of the latter occurred during the sinking of a ferry in the North Sea, where some of the survivors passed the time waiting to be rescued by singing a humorous song called 'Always Look on the Bright Side of Life'.

Fortunately, there are far more examples of spontaneous group singing that occur under pleasanter circumstances. Here are some examples:

- SING-ALONGS, such as in holiday coaches and pubs.
- CHILDREN'S SONGS AND RHYMES: These songs are usually learned at school, where children pass them on to new 'generations' of pupils. This is very similar to the oral (spoken) tradition that exists in cultures where songs and stories are passed down verbally rather than being written down. They can have a wide range of themes. One theme that often occurs is that of love and marriage (for example, 'Susie and

Slaves' work songs are one example of group singing under difficult or oppressive conditions.

Children's songs, games and education often involve group singing.

Johnny sitting in a tree, K-I-S-S-I-N-G'). Others have historical origins, such as 'Ring-a-Ring o' Roses' which, it is thought, may be about the plague – the line 'Atishoo! Atishoo! We all fall down!' is believed to be a rather grim reference to the sneezing fits that were one of the symptoms of the disease and to the patient's subsequent death. In cultures where it is acceptable, children are also taught group singing at school.

- AUDIENCE PARTICIPATION has a long history as a part of popular culture and there are many forms of musical entertainment where the audience is encouraged to join in as a group. One example is the music hall tradition, a form of variety show popular in Victorian Britain, similar to **vaudeville** in the USA. The audience is expected to know songs and choruses (these may be distributed on sheets of paper) and to join in as required. Interestingly, this also happens at rock concerts, where the audience is likely to sing along to songs they know, often encouraged to do so by the performers. This is generally taken to be a mark of the audience's support and enthusiasm, but if an audience were to do the same during, say, an **opera**, this would indicate insensitivity and a lack of appreciation for the music.

25

Solo and virtual groups

As discussed earlier (see page 6), even a single musician performing alone represents a whole group of people who have made the performance possible. Developments in technology, however, have made this into a much more direct process – a single musician can now make the kind of music normally associated with a group. But have all these new possibilities taken away the unique experience of making music in the company of other real human beings, though?

A 'one-man band' is a curious mixture of solo artist and group music.

Early developments

For one musician to be able to perform as a 'group', they must be able to artificially add to their abilities. Alternatively, they must have instruments that produce sound with little or no input by the musician. This is in fact a very old idea as there are many types of 'self-playing' instrument that date back to ancient times. Examples include the Aeolian harp, a stringed instrument which is placed outdoors so that the wind makes its strings **resonate**; wind chimes, which are often used as domestic ornaments; and water chimes, a traditional Japanese instrument with a delicate sound made by water dripping onto thin, flat surfaces. It is likely that human beings' first experiments with sound made use of other natural phenomena, such as the echo within a cave.

26

The poor sound quality of the first recorded music made it unsuitable for use in a performance situation – even radio broadcasting. However, an earlier and quite successful means of recording sound, specifically piano performances, was the player-piano. This system allowed 'recordings' to be made by a mechanism which would punch a hole in a roll of paper each time a note was played. This could then be 'played back' by the instrument, with the notes playing according to the positions of the holes. Many famous musicians, including the German composer Brahms (1837–1897), made piano rolls. Other 'low-tech' solutions include the one-man band – a single musician playing numerous instruments using straps, cables and levers; and the cinema organ, which allows a range of sounds from real instruments (such as cymbals and drums) to be played from a keyboard.

Technology and the virtual group

With the advent of modern instrument technology, it became possible for any musician to perform 'group music'. Some examples of this are:

- AUTO-ACCOMPANIMENT, PROGRAMMING AND SEQUENCING: Computers and keyboards can record several musical parts as **digital** data.
- MULTITRACKED RECORDING: A single musician can record several instrumental parts to make a multi-instrument **solo** recording.
- **DJ**ing AND REMIXING: A single DJ can create new pieces of music by mixing and remixing existing recordings.

The DJ has become an important figure in the modern music scene.

The future of group music-making

At the very beginning of group music-making and throughout its history one factor has remained constant. That is the obvious need for the people involved to cooperate and act together. A group of people needed to be organized in order to produce effective music. However, modern music technology and communications media such as the Internet would appear to have changed this.

Absentee musicians

While commercial recordings involving a number of musicians are presented as being the products of a concerted artistic effort on the part of all involved, this can often be a very false impression. The technology that allows each instrument and/or voice in a group to be recorded individually also provides opportunities to revise the music in different ways. It also allows individual parts to be recorded at different times and places. For example, if the members of a successful band all live in different countries they do not even need to gather in the same place to make their next hit record. They can record their parts separately and have the engineer and producer mix them at their leisure. This can result in a strange sort of musical group in which half the participants have never met the other half.

In the 1980s, music technology changed with the introduction of the compact disc. Nowadays you can download music directly from the Internet.

Sound sculptures

The UK group Echo City performs and creates 'community sound sculptures' making a kind of 'playground' full of **participatory** percussion instruments.

Unfeasibly perfect muscians

Digital editing can allow an entire musical part not just to be corrected, but also to be changed by the producer and engineer, so that any individual contribution to a group may end up sounding quite unlike the original intention.

No muscians

During the rise of disco in the 1980s, many opportunities for live music were lost, as venues were more willing to book **DJs** whose performances, being based on recorded music, were both simpler to stage and musically reliable. This caused many musicians to abandon live group music.

The new generation

However, group music making has cleverly sidestepped these problems. The Internet has provided the perfect means for musicians to exchange information, with worldwide communication now being the norm. Community-based bands and orchestras are stronger than ever and live group music flourishes in non-**Western** cultures. New types of live performance groups have arisen, mixing music with dance, theatre or community activities in ways which cannot be replaced by technology. It seems that the need to make music together will always be with us.

Glossary

acoustic referring to sound; also means unamplified

acoustic swing a type of popular music, related to jazz, which features unamplified instruments

alto a high male voice; used of instruments such as a saxophones, it means lower in pitch than soprano

amplify/amplification to make louder

baritone a pitch range (and name for a singing voice) higher than bass but lower than tenor

bass the lowest range of notes in general use

bodhran an Irish folk drum

bongos a pair of small hand drums widely used in Latin and Afro-Cuban music

bouzouki a Greek fretted stringed instrument

choral describes music performed by a group of singers

civilian not belonging to the armed forces

close-harmonies singing where each voice sings a melody close to but complementing the others

composition a piece of written music

concertina a hand-held reed instrument operated by bellows

congas large hand drums used mainly in Latin and Afro-Cuban music

contemporary of the present day

contralto the pitch range (and name for a singing voice) above alto and below treble

cowbells hollow metal percussion instruments played with sticks which are widely used in Latin music but also in other musical forms

digital using a computer type 'language' of electronic ones and zeros

diversity a wide variety of something

DJ from 'disc jockey' – a performer who plays and mixes music from recordings

dynamics whether music is quiet or loud

ensemble a musical performing group which is smaller than an orchestra

fantastical related to or influenced by fantasy

glockenspiel a percussion instrument which consists of tuned metal bars which are played with beaters

in tune said of an instrument which has been adjusted to produce notes which are accurate in pitch and which match those of any other instruments being played

indigenous native to a particular area

kazoo an instrument which makes a sound by modifying the player's voice with a vibrating membrane

key the group of notes used in a piece of music, based on a chosen scale and named after the first note of that scale, e.g. the key of C

lute an early fretted stringed instrument

melody the main tune in a piece of music

muted reducing the sound made by an instrument

opera a form of theatrical performance in which all the words are sung, usually to orchestral accompaniment

participatory describes an activity which people are allowed to take part in

percussionist a musician who plays percussion instruments

pitch how high or low a note is

predator an animal which hunts others for food

prehistoric before history was formally recorded

prey animals caught for food

range the total number of notes an instrument or voice can reach, from the lowest to the highest

reed a strip of cane which vibrates when air is blown across it

repertoire the collection of musical pieces written for or played by a person or musical group

resonate to vibrate in the presence of sound

rhythm the time, pulse and beat of music; use of time in music

samba an Afro-Cuban form of music and dance

score a musical composition, including all the instrumental and vocal parts, written down as sheet music

semi-pitched drum a drum which can be tuned higher or lower but which does not have a clearly defined note

solo a section of music or a composition which features a single musician, or which is played by one musician alone

soprano normally the highest instrument or voice

tempering refers to the adjustment of the sound by heating and hammering during manufacture

tenor an instrument or voice which is lower than alto but higher than baritone

timbales single-headed drums, usually made of metal and played with thin sticks, which are used in Afro-Cuban music

timbre the distinctiveness of a sound

timpani large single-headed drums with copper shells used mainly in classical music

tone the quality of a sound, usually described in visual terms – bright, dark, thin etc.

treble a pitch range (and name for a singing voice) above contralto and below soprano

tremolo a rapid variation in the loudness of a sound

tube resonators cylindrical tubes found on some percussion instruments which make the sound of the instrument louder

vaudeville entertainment on-stage featuring music and comedy acts

virtuosity exceptional instrumental ability

vocal to do with the voice and/or singing

West/ern these terms are used by musicologists to distinguish the music of Europe and the English-speaking countries from that of the rest of the world

woodblocks percussion instruments made of wood, with slots cut in them which act as resonators

Index

Titles in the *Soundbites* series include:

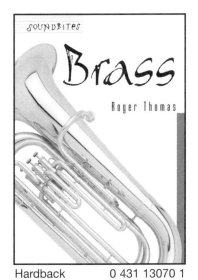

Hardback   0 431 13070 1

Hardback   0 431 13071 X

Hardback   0 431 13072 8

Hardback   0 431 13073 6

Hardback   0 431 13074 4

Hardback   0 431 13075 2

Find out about the other titles in this series on our website www.heinemann.co.uk/library